Back in Harvest Town

poems by

Allen M Weber

Finishing Line Press
Georgetown, Kentucky

Back in Harvest Town

ACKNOWLEDGMENTS

Grateful acknowledgment is made to the following publications in which
some of these poems first appeared:

Autumn Skies: "Cliffhanger"
The Daily Press:" Still Life"
Fourth River: "Lake Michigan Boys"
Haunted Waters Press: "Chickadee"
Loch Raven Review: "The Borrow Pit," "Estate Sale," and "To be wild"
Terrain: "The Lingering Sound of Skipping Stones," "Migration North," and
"Tributaries"
Unlikely Stories: "Leaving Harvest Town"
The Esthetic Apostle: "Storm Chasers"

Publisher: Leah Huete de Maines
Editor: Christen Kincaid
Cover Art: Allen M Weber
Author Photo: Tracy Rice Weber
Cover Design: Elizabeth Maines McCleavy

Order online: www.finishinglinepress.com
also available on amazon.com

Author inquiries and mail orders:
Finishing Line Press
PO Box 1626
Georgetown, Kentucky 40324
USA

Contents

Lake Michigan Boys 1

Cliffhanger 2

The Borrow Pit 3

Leaving Harvest Town 4

Storm Chasers 5

Hardwood Autumn 6

Melody 7

Domestic 8

Estate Sale 9

Mood Indigo 10

Chickadee 11

Care of the Weeping Cherry 12

Still Life 13

Sitting with my wife on the couch 14

Migration North 15

We Children of Angeline 16

Will and Testament 17

Tributaries 18

To be wild 19

Solstice 20

The Lingering Sound of Skipping Stones 21

So we are grasped by what we cannot grasp;

—*Rainer Maria Rilke*

Lake Michigan Boys

Winter never lifts suddenly.
Creeping temperatures tease

groaning fissures into the ice,
and sometimes a cocksure boy

wanders too far from shore
to make an island of himself.

His friends, aground and enflamed
with indecision, watch him grow

smaller, as he drifts away
on that breakaway floe.

Once, we were Spartan—
AM radio and cut-off jeans.

Coastal girls would wriggle free
from winter coats, then from summer

shifts, to gambol barely out of reach
of the cold and muttering surf.

Prone with elbows and loins
pressed into the warming sand,

we'd confront their sun-washed skin,
speak up or ache like a tooth.

Cliffhanger

Clinging to this rocky shelf—Lucidity—
with no jutting branch for a craven change
of mind, the impact promises to be famous—

a mushroom splash, while zombies line the edge
to gawp. They'd have me tumble back like balsa
on a whitecap. It's expected to be so spurned—

to be ordinary—I don't much care for it.
Nothing happens here that begs description.
But really, I don't like to complain.

The Borrow Pit

When Earle would say, Need you, Little Bro, I'd always come
running—that's the way it was. On a visit home from the Navy,
he tells a tale of swimming from torpedo tubes, how his men
take fear to folk you'd never read about in the Daily Gazette.

Growing up, Earle could tread water forever—had to be tough
in the pit by the blueberry fields: the water gets dark, real fast;
the steep mud bottom tricks your feet, so there's no way to rest.
A neighbor boy drowned there—cramped up, maybe, slipping

right under, no chance to call for his friends. We weren't allowed,
but some nights we'd sneak down, with a six-pack, to skinny-dip
till the farmer's hounds got to howling and we'd know that soon
the screen door would bang shut, and we'd see his flatbed Ford

as bouncing balls of light, clattering down the dusty path. Tonight
a black Buick glides in—*One Nation Under a Groove* and something
like joy pulsing from the open windows—some city boys muling
uncut coke from Chicago. I take one look at Earle—those blue lips,

how they stretch across his berry-stained teeth, and even before
he lifts the grocery bag of money and glinting metal from the trunk,
I understand: not everybody's leaving this field tonight. Then Earle
tosses a shotgun and laughs, Hey Brother, still like to climb trees?

The sentinel maple quivers and startles my skin with an earlier rain.
Hugging a lower branch, oiled steel ices my cheek. Between leaves
I make out that Earle's showing off—got all three flocked together,
bowed down and kneeling, facing the edge of his still moon water.

Leaving Harvest Town

About a crime how town council had our overpass repainted,
denying the high impact graffito splashed beside the archway
below the rails—testament so sublime that paint-can-wielding
juveniles refused to blaspheme with mere hearts and letters.

A jovial teen—call him Hero—had a high-stepping faith
that just happens when Daddy's rich and Mama's good looking.
Remember parties where he'd dance across the grass and twirl
an auntie—*You Ain't Seen Nothing Yet*, booming from an 8 track.

Then there was Leanne. Her razor tongue left most boys dumb,
but a misfortune of tousled hair and caramel skin—smooth
over newly ripened curves—compelled a weathered man
to abandon his orchards and gather her with peach-stone hands.

Suppose they're still delicious—tales of that windfall girl
and the farmer who won't buy groceries in his hometown
anymore. When fruit is fallen, damaged, folk around here,
they're pretty quick to press it into cider. Anyway,

losing Leanne sure drove our Hero hard—better than 60
according to the rubber crescents burned onto the pavement
as he hugged that curve just past the volunteer fire station.
Buckets of paint in the truck's bed, he pushed the pedal down

one last time—Abuela's house a blur to his left. Lurching
over the curb, he slammed three shades of blue into the concrete,
leaving not one hint of exclamation mark on his last stretch
of road, to help us all believe he could've changed his mind.

Storm Chasers

Even in his dreams she'd not surrender
herself to him. But sometimes her blouse,
cotton white, would melt away in the rain.

Like her mother, she'd one day race ahead,
change her name, and marry a landed bastard,
before drinking herself to death. Enduring

a mother skunk's last defiance, she wiped a tear
from her eye and pedaled past the crushed remains.
Beside the potholed road, a killdeer feigned

an injured wing as Mike stopped to save the kit
left wailing in the briars. He smoothed her fur—
black, cleaved by stripes of white—then sheltered her

beneath his shirt. Standing on his pedals, Mike
tried to close the gap Mel opened between them.
He glimpsed her bike in the shivering grass

at the base of the water tower,
and Mel, climbing rung after rusted rung
into the marbled gray and yellow sky.

Swooning over the view, he ascended
to find her amid the tumult she'd sought.
At the catwalk, wind rumbled like a train.

The storm pummeled the empty iron reservoir—
an abandoned timpani thrummed by hail.
Rows of hard green apples bobbed below.

Mel teetered on the handrail—bare feet
kicking electrified air above the chasm.
She applauded the funnel as it turned

her father's roof to swirling debris. Her hair
whipped Mike's face as he encircled her waist
to trust the orphaned skunk into her hands.

Hardwood Autumn

Abiding more when out of doors (or well into his drink),
Big Mike takes the better part of a day to harvest half
a dozen rows. His John Deere idles near the yellow-leafed copse,

where at twelve years old they covered hickory nuts with loam—
he and that pretty neighbor who, at sixteen, married quick
some blue-eyed boy whose daddy owned a Chevy dealership.

Mike spies his Carmen yanking boxers from the line, clothespins
tumbling to the grass. Tonight he'll face reprisal meatloaf,
without complaint—or salt. He'll share with her the phantom

deer: each fall, they graze the edge of harrowed fields, white tails
like flags as they bound away. Won't be a lie. Should've seen 'em,
Carm. Dove into them woods like children into a black-water pond.

Melody

Providence held her to orchard paths, dropped
a match in that house where nobody lived.
Having stayed one year a ghost, only
a Unitarian choir would suffer her leaving.

Wading gravel streams and asphalt rivers,
she washed into the depot to find what passage
her savings might afford. A gust stole lyrics
from a troubadour's hand; they cartwheeled

across the yellow line, past a mandolin case—
open at her feet. No coquette, she looked down
to smooth her fluttering dress—robin's-egg
blue—just so, by God, they never met.

Domestic

Her dress drapes a ladderback chair. Unpinned, her hair
sweeps the flour-dusted butcher block. Released for now,
her grateful breasts rebound from every straight-arm thrust.
She's kneaded and covered mounds of dough; they're left to rise.

Hens cackle in the yard. Through the window she takes
a trembling aim, mouthing, *Bang. Bang.* Two town boys fall
behind tall grass at the edge of the road, still living
to harass her chickens with their sticks and stones.

She punches down the yeasty balls (so they may rise again),
and tells the cat of slights and crisply ironed shirts—
her words so hot, the tabby flees her square of sun
that warms the beaten heartwood pine. The floor replies

as she shifts her burden, foot to calloused foot. She spies
her husband and son, returning from a distant field.
The lengths of their strides measure out her time to re-dress,
wring a rooster's neck, and wipe the mess from her hands.

Estate Sale

Bargain hunters and the merely curious will gather here
like crows. More pieces of Elna's life will be carried off
like still-warm roadkill. Each sale is final, a curative necessity
to fund a sun-filled, dry-air retirement home in Arizona.

Michigan winters come harsh, and for another spring, the fields
lie unturned. Too faded to fill the buoyant saffron dress, fanned
across her bed, or to help daffodils prevail against overrunning
weeds, she cannot hope to keep fusty air from vacant rooms.

And everyone knows how it was the indivisible Fred and Freddie
who ran the farm. Fred, the only man to ever make her feel safe.
And Freddie—autistic before we knew what autism was—could
build an engine and squeeze sweet measures from his accordion

with equal skill. In the space of a year, Freddie followed Fred
to an adjacent family plot. So Elna's touched by a merciful god,
relieving her of sentimentality for nouns and tender obligation
to stay for a son whose only answer was a whisper, *I miss my dad.*

Mood Indigo

Like a blue flame in a speakeasy,
that's how Grandpa found her,
shuddering and swaying to *Mood Indigo*.
But family lore does not explain
what a hard-handed man could say
that would make a woman like her trade
uptown celebrity for orchards and fields—

∞

the glamor of tending endless rows.
Seventy-two years later, her mind's tripped
back to Chicago. Having met again
the warmest man, she's boxed everything she owns
and put on that old blue dress. Through the screen,
I see her rocking on the front porch swing,
waiting to ride to where she already is.

Chickadee

In the sudden night before the storm, a banditry foraged
beneath a low ceiling of marbled clouds—a sky that has you
take stock of your losses. We sorted through a box of letters
and photographs, considering the history of each.

Oak popped and whined in the woodstove. My wife paused,
solemn with a picture—my brother, on his final visit. In fading
color, black cap awry, he's still hand-in-hand with our sons,
racing headlong to somewhere beyond the focus of my lens.

How quickly snow covers the seeds that towhees scatter
to the ground. I went outside to fill the feeder. A windfall
chickadee, deceived by the light from our kitchen, fluttered
against the window, until, worn out, he let himself fall.

I pressed my finger against his breast. He hopped on, tilted
his black-capped head and fluffed against the cold.
Weary one, the darkness bewilders us all. I'll shelter you
in the holly hedge; by now an owl is watching from the barn.

Care of the Weeping Cherry

More deeply rooted, now it can stand alone.
Brother, I've come to remove the ties

from your memorial tree. Early blooms
are a pale pink beneath last night's dusting of snow.

This morning smells of loam. A chickadee
tilts his head, and watches from the fence.

Still Life

One should sympathise with the colour, the beauty, the joy of life.
~ Oscar Wilde

She brings no more persimmons to our door.
I hope we've not offended Mrs. Kim
with some American inattention.

Maybe her crop was taken by disease,
or stress, induced by August drought, compelled
her trees to drop their still-green progeny.

Perhaps she'd view aesthetics as a waste:
Despite our curiosity, not one
persimmon passed our lips; still I'd insist

they were delicious. My painterly wife
presents our fruit to morning light, just so
we sympathize with still ripening hues.

And then we dither—salsa, chutney, cake?—
while flesh goes soft, skin wrinkles, juices slake
the bottom of our cherished earthen bowl.

Sitting with my wife on the couch

There's not one child in the room.
A cardinal has finally braved the feeder
by the window. The azaleas are lighted
more perfectly than they might be
even a moment from now. I think
it would be okay if we were to stay
like this for just a little bit longer.

Migration North

I helped my grandma down the salted walk,
into the van that Uncle Dallas warmed
ten minutes ago. I laid the hickory cane
across her lap, kissed her cheek, and told her
I loved her before sliding shut the door.

My wife has given to me a family
tradition of watching departing guests—
waving until they're out of sight—a rite
of Southern courtesy and contemplation
I practice now without a coat or hat.

I'll wait till distance veils the engine's hum
and I can hear the murmur of my heart.
Lake-effect snow tumbles, melts on my face;
another cloud—swirling silver—envelops
a moment, Venus and the waxing moon.

In shared stillness, the wilder residents
of our refuge—Canadian geese and
mallards—huddle in bulrush near the lake
where the ice is thin. Each has reason
to endure the splendor of wintering here.

Consider the peevish pair of mute swans:
the cob, waving a mangled wing, postures
and hisses to shield his pen. Why does she
prolong the myth of swan monogamy?
By acts, not reason, she's most inspired.

By the fire, my Virginia girl enthralls
her grateful in-laws with musical wit.
Laughter rises with smoke from the chimney.
I wave as the taillights wink and dissolve
into a far copse of blue, snow-lit spruce.

We Children of Angeline

Great grandmother bestowed them with a quest.
My boys peer down a woodchuck hole between
the maple roots of family lore, the same that pushed
the cover from this tomb, one hundred years ago.

Two teens, who dared to reach inside and brush her cheek,
declared their Grandma Angeline looked just the same
as when they sat upon her knee, except she'd turned
dark and hard as the granite slab that marks her grave.

But those young men grew old before my birth.
No living heir can say her bathing brook still flows,
or knows what trick she used to sweeten wild berry
pies—baked for children of the Potawatomi.

Did she arrive by ox-drawn cart—red hair spilling
from an Irish bonnet? Perhaps she answered once
to a Pokagon name, her skin the color of
late autumn leaves. On weather-punished stone,

the chiseled text has worn shallow, yet we can feel
the Angel letters of her name. This field is filled
with kin who've thrived as branches from her life.

If we listen to the rustled leaves,
maybe we'll hear a future child repeat
the legend of our passing once this way.

Will and Testament

After her diagnosis—stage 4,
too late for chemo—Mom staked

saplings on a hill. How will they
survive disease and grazing deer,

without mortal devotion,
the nurturing presence of

the orchardist? She told me,
I should go outside. Look at them.

But it was raining, and besides,
I thought it wise not to stray

too far from her side. I failed her,
once again missing the point.

How long will it take to realize
the harvest she foresaw?

Some distant, crisp autumn, a son,
a daughter may come to find her

beloved orioles in laden branches.
Foraging the windfall, a doe

will toss her head and stamp the earth,
nostrils flaring at the intrusion.

Still, they who see her would say
that she was unafraid.

Tributaries

Talked to your mama at the grocery store—
tried to slip by me in the canned soup aisle.
She said you'd married. Sold the horses. Moved
north, where hardwoods line the Escanaba.

Back home, an orange X dooms our maple.
Wrapped in an Indian blanket—still damp
with the syrupy scent of your mare—we
made silly promises beneath its canopy.

My father, laid off from the GM plant,
sold the back thirty to a logging firm.
They've dozed an earthen bridge—a portage
for harvesters, a dead end for salmon.

Remember that forty-pounder pulled
from Black River?—a male, hens followed, fat
with roe. We ran for the mist of the falls,
cheering their whitewater leaps toward home.

Snowmelt gorged our secret creek. River-wide,
it split the old growth woods; the shallows churned
so red with Chinook, we'd a notion to
trip bank to bank across their gleaming backs.

To Be Wild

Is that rumble from these passing clouds?
No, it's half a ton of evocative beast
snorting and charging—a conceivable clash.

With you, lovely son, on my shoulders
and so many steps to the paddock fence,
I wrench about in loose, suburban shoes

to face the storm of hooves; I glower
and growl: Whoa! Stomping to a stop
he dips and tosses his head. Generous

with humor, you laugh, reaching for the softness
of his flaring nose. Ah, he's still a colt!—
I'd forgotten how it is to be wild.

Solstice

Will you swim with me, Dad?

Beneath the humid moon,
he's somersaulted—barely a splash.

Did you see me, Dad? Watch this, Dad!

In the deepening prism of the pool, my son
suspends himself, like a mayfly in amber.
We celebrate the longest day well into the night.

Hazy summers ago, I too
held my breath, and kicked my feet
beneath a flickering surface—reflections
blazing with lakeside bonfires.

Jump in, Dad. The water's warm, Dad.

Sinking to the cool mud bottom, weeds
encircle my ankles. Lungs
burn for air.

Still my father waits for me to surface.
He's my lighthouse at the end of the dock—
the cherry of his cigar glowing, fading,
glowing, again.

The Lingering Sounds of Skipping Stones

He sits on the hood of his rented car,
and breezes come remembered, redolent
with coconut lotions and stranded alewife.

As they always have, lovers weave
between the last fishermen on the pier,
or wade ankle-deep in the surf.

Boats retire from the freshwater horizon—
sway, marina bound, down Black River.
He remembers a young woman hiking

her summer dress to run through the sedge.
Her legs scissor, silhouetted in orange light.
Her toes throw the cooling sand—

skip—step—pivot—toss—

as the sun loses interest in another day;
in descent, its arc briefly flames
the side-armed stone. Flat and tumbled

smooth, it breaks the tension of the surface
again and again and again; winking,
concentric eyes fade into the swells.

A younger man lifts her shadow
to his shoulders. The joy of living.
Their laughter echoes like bells.

And as they always have, the gulls
mock cries of mirth or sadness
as they navigate the fading heat.

Allen M Weber lives in Hampton, Virginia with his poet wife and two of their three sons. His poems have appeared in numerous journals and anthologies—including *Arc Poetry, Changing Harm to Harmony: Bullies and Bystanders Project, The Chronicle of Higher Education, Naugatuck River Review, A Prairie Home Companion, Sequestrum* and *Splash!—Haunted Waters Press.*

www.ingramcontent.com/pod-product-compliance
Lightning Source LLC
Chambersburg PA
CBHW022104080426
42734CB00009B/1484